A Note to Parents

DK READERS is a compelling program for beginning readers, designed in conjunction with leading literacy experts, including Dr. Linda Gambrell, Director of the Eugenge T. Moore School of Education at Clemson University. Dr. Gambrell has served on the Board of Directors of the International Reading Association and as President of the National Reading Conference.

Beautiful illustrations and superb full-color photographs combine with engaging, easy-to-read stories to offer a fresh approach to each subject in the series. Each DK READER is guaranteed to capture a child's interest while developing his or her reading skills, general knowledge, and love of reading.

The five levels of DK READERS are aimed at different reading abilities, enabling you to choose the books that are exactly right for your child:

Pre-level 1: Learning to read
Level 1: Beginning to read
Level 2: Beginning to read alone
Level 3: Reading alone
Level 4: Proficient readers

The "normal" age at which a child begins to read can be anywhere from three to eight years old, so these levels are only a general guideline.

No matter which level you select, you can be sure that you are helping your child learn to read, then read to learn!

LONDON, NEW YORK, MUNICH,
MELBOURNE, AND DELHI

Series Editor Deborah Lock
Art Editor Sadie Thomas
U.S. Editor Elizabeth Hester
Production Shivani Pandey
DTP Designer Almudena Díaz
Jacket Designer Simon Oon
Photographer Andy Crawford

Reading Consultant
Linda Gambrell, Ph.D.

First American Edition, 2004
04 05 06 07 08 10 9 8 7 6 5 4 3 2 1
Published in the United States by DK Publishing, Inc.
375 Hudson Street, New York, New York 10014

Published in Great Britain by Dorling Kindersley Limited

Library of Congress Cataloging-in-Publication Data
Lock, Deborah.
  A trip to the library / written by Deborah Lock.-- 1st American ed.
  p. cm. -- (DK readers)
  Summary: Lauren and her mother visit the library to find out what
  there is to do in their new town, and are introduced to the building
    and its services by their new neighbor, Dan.
  ISBN 0-7566-0277-7 (PB) -- ISBN 0-7566-0278-5 (PLC)
  [1. Libraries--Fiction. 2. Books and reading--Fiction. 3. Moving,
  Household--Fiction.] I. Title. II. Dorling Kindersley readers.
PZ7.L7858Tri 2004
[E]--dc22
                          2003026612

Color reproduction by Colourscan, Singapore
Printed and bound in China by L Rex Printing Co., Ltd.

Photographs taken at Brompton Library
with thanks to Angela Goreham and staff;
and the entrance of Victoria Library
Thanks also to all the models: Rhianna Stamps, Caroline Stamps,
Che Commerasamy Bryers from Scallywags,
Rochea Brown, Gabby Stamps, and Anil Thomas

All other images © Dorling Kindersley Limited
For further information see: www.dkimages.com

Discover more at
www.dk.com

DK READERS

BEGINNING 1 TO READ

A Trip to the Library

Written by Deborah Lock

DK Publishing, Inc.

Lauren and her family moved to a new town. "What is there to do here?" asked Lauren.

"We can visit the local library," said Mom.

At the library, Lauren met Dan, her new neighbor.

"Hi, Lauren," called Dan.

"I come to the library all the time. I'll show you around."

At the front desk, Dan handed some books to the librarian.

librarian

"I'm returning these books,"
said Dan, "but I'd like to renew
this one, please."

The librarian
checked in the books
with a scanner.

scanner

She gave Dan the book
he wanted to read again.

"Where can I become a member of the library?" asked Lauren.
"At the help desk,"
said the librarian.

At the help desk, Lauren and Mom gave their names and new address to another librarian.

They were given
their own library cards.
The librarian told them
about the library.
"We are here to help," she said.

Dan and Lauren went
to the children's area.
Each shelf was filled with books.

"I like reading about animals," said Lauren, "but where will I find books about them?"

shelf

"Here they are," said Dan,
pointing to some shelves.
"Books about animals
are all together."

"I'll choose some books,"
said Lauren.

Meanwhile, Mom went
to the adults' area.
She looked at the display
of new books.
She read the back covers
of the books to find out
more about the stories.

"It's story time," said the librarian. Dan and Lauren sat on the bench to listen to the story.

bench

It was a tale about
a lion and a mouse.

"Now you can make some
animal masks," said the librarian.
Dan made
a lion mask with
an orange mane.

mask

Lauren made some fluffy ears
for her mouse mask.

"I'd like to borrow the story time book," said Lauren. "Are there any copies on the shelves?"

computer

"We can search for the title
on the computer," replied Dan.
"You can also use
the Internet here."

There was one copy of
the story book in the library.
Lauren found it and then
looked at the other
picture books.

"We can choose video tapes and story tapes, too," said Dan.

video tape

Lauren found Mom looking at
the notice boards.
"I'm finding out about things to do
in the area," said Mom.

"Can I borrow these books and tapes?" asked Lauren.
"Yes," said Mom.
"Let's go to the exit desk."

The librarian scanned
Lauren's library card and
then the books and tapes.

She stamped
the return date
on them.
"Please return them
in three weeks,"
she said.

stamp

"Thanks," said Lauren.
"I'll come again soon."

31

Picture word list

librarian

page 8

mask

page 22

scanner

page 10

computer

page 24

shelf

page 15

video tape

page 27

bench

page 20

stamp

page 30